Academic Writing:
As Easy AS 1, 2, 3

by J. Nathan Garrett, MA

Academic Writing: As Easy As 1-2-3 by J. Nathan Garrett

ISBN: 9798372007642

Cover and interior designed by VINCO
For inquiries: h2mcreatives@gmail.com

TABLE OF CONTENTS

Academic Writing: As Easy As 1-2-3 by J. Nathan Garrett

INTRODUCTION

Academic writing is scary to lots of students. It doesn't need to be.

Even if you don't really understand what a thesis statement is or topic sentences are or you're not sure how to order your thoughts or even come up with thoughts – that's all right. This simple workbook is going to help you learn to build your academic writing simply and with very little stress.

That's right, we said 'build.' Because it's true! Academic writing has two phases – the first draft and the revisions. The initial drafting is entirely about building your essay. You don't even need to think about it in terms of 'writing' yet. Writing happens during the revisions phase.

We'll start with a visual of what your academic essay should look like. The visual will be on one page – but that doesn't mean the essay you put together will be only one page. The visual we show you is the overall structure of the essay, be it one page, three pages, or even your doctoral dissertation!

Okay, actually, doctoral dissertations are a different animal altogether.

After the visual breakdown, we'll do a couple fun brainstorming exercises, then jump right into creating thesis statements. Creating thesis statements is what we call an 'iterative process.' Which means you could be changing your thesis statement right up until the very end of building and revising your essay! That's all right. The goal is to create a thesis statement that provides guidance on what your essay is focused on. We have several worksheets that will help you learn to craft killer thesis statements faster than you can imagine.

Once we have a good thesis statement, we'll get going on your introduction, body paragraphs, and conclusion. The thesis statement is *key* to getting the rest of those going in the right direction, so we'll spend enough time to help you really get it right.

Let's go!

Academic Writing: As Easy As 1-2-3 by J. Nathan Garrett

STRUCTURE OF AN ACADEMIC ESSAY (VISUAL)

Introduction

Hook

**Context that transitions from
Hook to Thesis Statement**

**Thesis statement (with
main points)**

Body

Body Paragraph 1

1. Topic sentence (refer directly to first main point mentioned in the thesis statement)
2. Support 1 (can be one sentence or more)
3. Support 2 (can be one sentence or more)
4. Support 3 (if needed, can be one sentence or more)
5. Concluding sentence that drives the point home

Body Paragraph 2

1. Topic sentence (refer directly to second main point mentioned in the thesis statement)
2. Support 1 (can be one sentence or more)
3. Support 2 (can be one sentence or more)
4. Support 3 (if needed, can be one sentence or more)
5. Concluding sentence that drives the point home

Body Paragraph 3

1. Topic sentence (refer directly to third main point mentioned in the thesis statement)
2. Support 1 (can be one sentence or more)
3. Support 2 (can be one sentence or more)
4. Support 3 (if needed, can be one sentence or more)
5. Concluding sentence that drives the point home

Restate thesis

Restate your main points/arguments

Conclusion

Conclude with a final, impactful insight

Academic Writing: As Easy As 1-2-3 by J. Nathan Garrett

BRAINSTORMING

Brainstorming works best when you do exactly what the word says: let your brain storm! Or in other words, free write whatever comes to mind.

Go! Start freewriting anything that comes to mind right now.

Go on.

Are you asking "About what?" If so, that's normal and is exactly right. Brainstorming about any old random thing doesn't work. Instead, we need to give the storm in our brains a direction to move so that we can actually be productive.

Here are some steps for brainstorming. We will follow these steps with a few useful brainstorming exercises, including graphic organizers, that can help the storms in our brains be even more productive.

Steps for Brainstorming

Step 1: Make sure you set enough time aside for your brainstorming. Plan on five to ten minutes or more.

Step 2: At the top of your page, be it paper or electronic, put the purpose of the essay you are supposed to write, along with any initial topic areas that have either been given to you or seem interesting to you. So if your class is about World History over the last fifty years, and you've been asked to write about an event that you think is important, write something like, "Important Events in the Last 50 Years" at the top of your page.

Step 3: Without letting yourself stop, write down as many ideas that come to you about your essay topic. Make a list with space under each idea. These are your topic ideas.

Step 4: When you run out of steam on Step 3, immediately go back and start writing ideas under each of the topic ideas. These are your sub-topics, or main ideas about each one. If you need to look something up while you do this, go

Academic Writing: As Easy As 1-2-3 by J. Nathan Garrett

ahead. Don't get distracted by an internet hole! And make sure you record where you got the information from so that you can build your bibliography.

Step 5: Now go back and see if there are some topic ideas that feel more interesting to you than the other ones. Circle or highlight them. Don't erase or delete your other material!

Step 6: Fill in any gaps or missing things in your favorite topic ideas. You can add more main ideas or more details about your main ideas. This is another great time to look things up. Remember: no internet holes and capture your sources. And stay away from Instagram, except for maybe a quick selfie of you working hard, then put your phone away until you're done.

Asking 'Wh' questions is a great way to fill gaps, or to even find them. Ask "Why?" "Who?" "What happened?" "When?" and "Where?" to add more details.

Step 7: By now, you probably have a feeling about one or two topic ideas you might want to write about. If you don't care, choose the one that seems most interesting or least boring.

Now it's time to move on to brainstorming exercises, including graphic organizers, so that we can flesh out our ideas and start to see how to structure our essay.

Brainstorming Exercises
Word Association
This is a basic exercise that is meant to get your brain going. You free-write any word that comes to mind as being associated with another word, phrase, or idea. For example, if you have to write a persuasive essay on the topic of your choosing, you could get started by doing this word association:

I have to persuade, because I'm right.   *Midnights*
Right…   *Anti-hero*
left   *I'm the problem*
movies   *oldies*
music   *classic music*
Taylor Swift

Academic Writing: As Easy As 1-2-3 by J. Nathan Garrett

By doing some word association we started thinking about how much we love Taylor Swift. So maybe our persuasive essay topic could be on why Taylor Swift is the most important musician recording music today.

Word association can get your brainstorming started. Once you think you want to write about Taylor Swift, you can follow the brainstorming steps we went over earlier to figure out what you'll include.

Graphic Organizers (Mind Mapping and Ven Diagrams)
Mind Mapping
Mind mapping is when you organize ideas and details in a way that shows relationship and hierarchy. It can be a great way to brainstorm and also start organizing your ideas – all at once. Here's a great example of mind mapping:

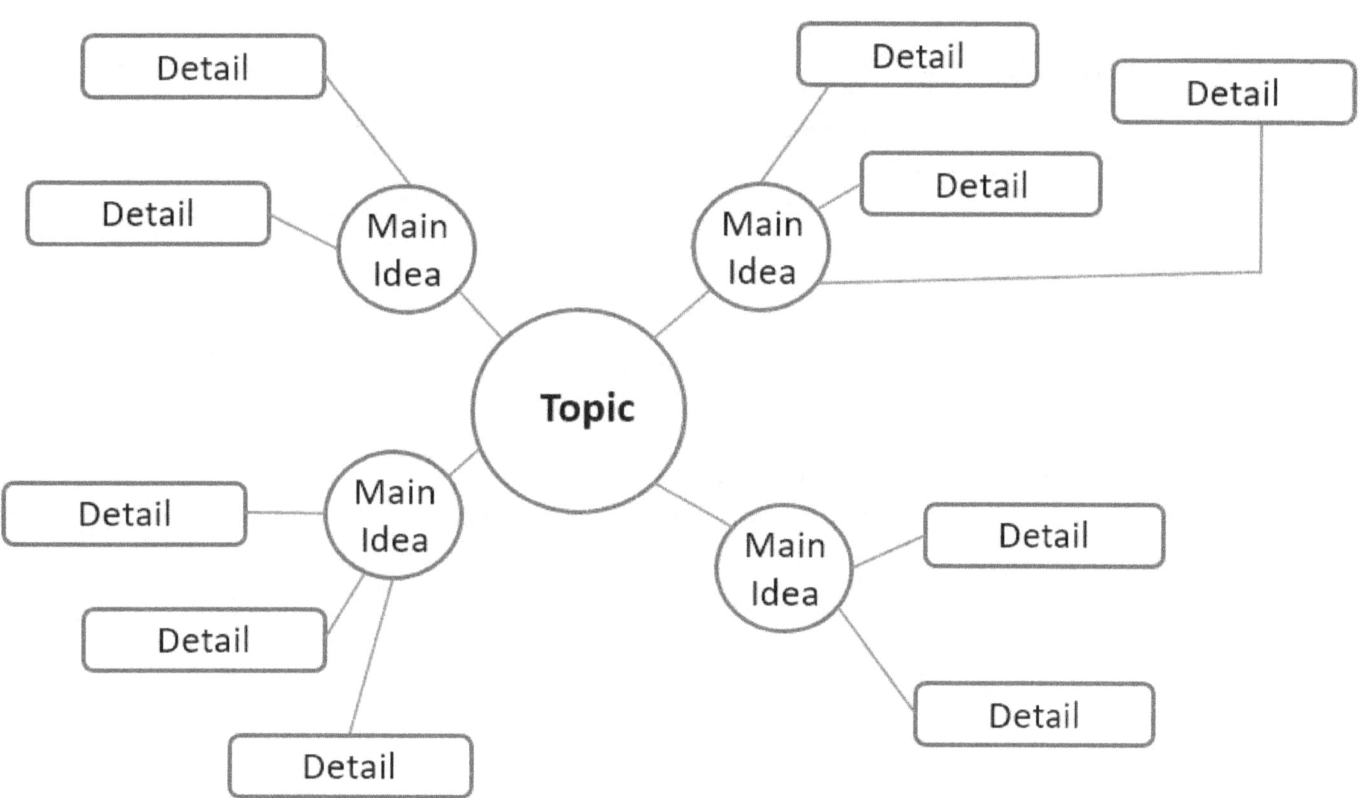

Academic Writing: As Easy As 1-2-3 by J. Nathan Garrett

In the mind map above, you would put the topic you've decided to write about in the circle in the middle, then add three or four, maybe even more, main ideas that are connected to that topic. Then draw some lines out from your main ideas and add details.

Making your mind map attractive like the beautiful one above is not necessary. Letting your brain get to work as you come up with ideas and organize them is how to get this done effectively.

Ven Diagrams
You've probably seen a Ven diagram before. This is a graphic organizer that shows the relations, or even logical commonalities, amongst sets. Ven diagrams can have two or more circles that overlap partly, and the information inside the overlapping portions are the shared details or commonalities.

Here's an example:

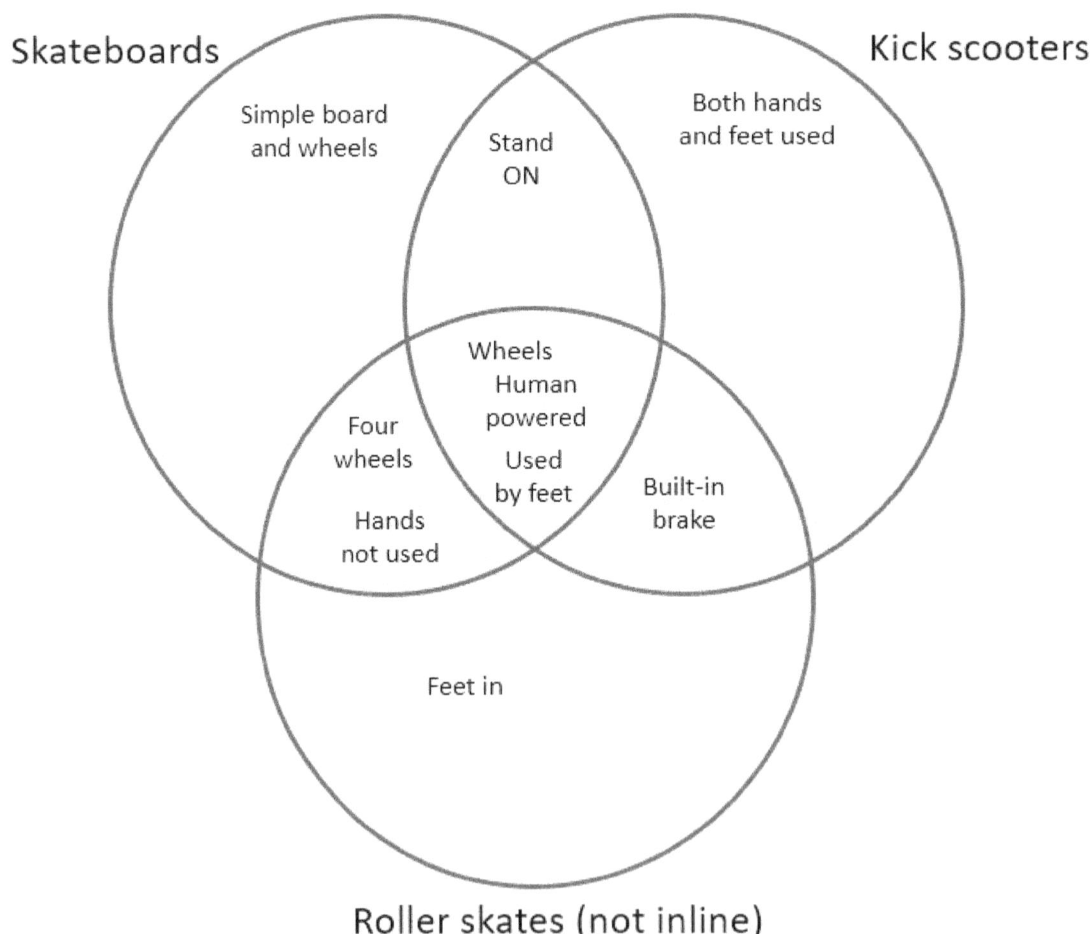

Can you think of any other details that are shared or not shared amongst skates, skateboards, and kick scooters? Go ahead and fill those in!

Do you see how powerful these graphic organizers can be? If you put enough work into fleshing out these organizers, you will find that you are better able to build your academic essay with greater ease.

Our next step is thesis statements. But first, the next two pages will have blank versions of the graphic organizers included above so that you can print them and use them as much as you need.

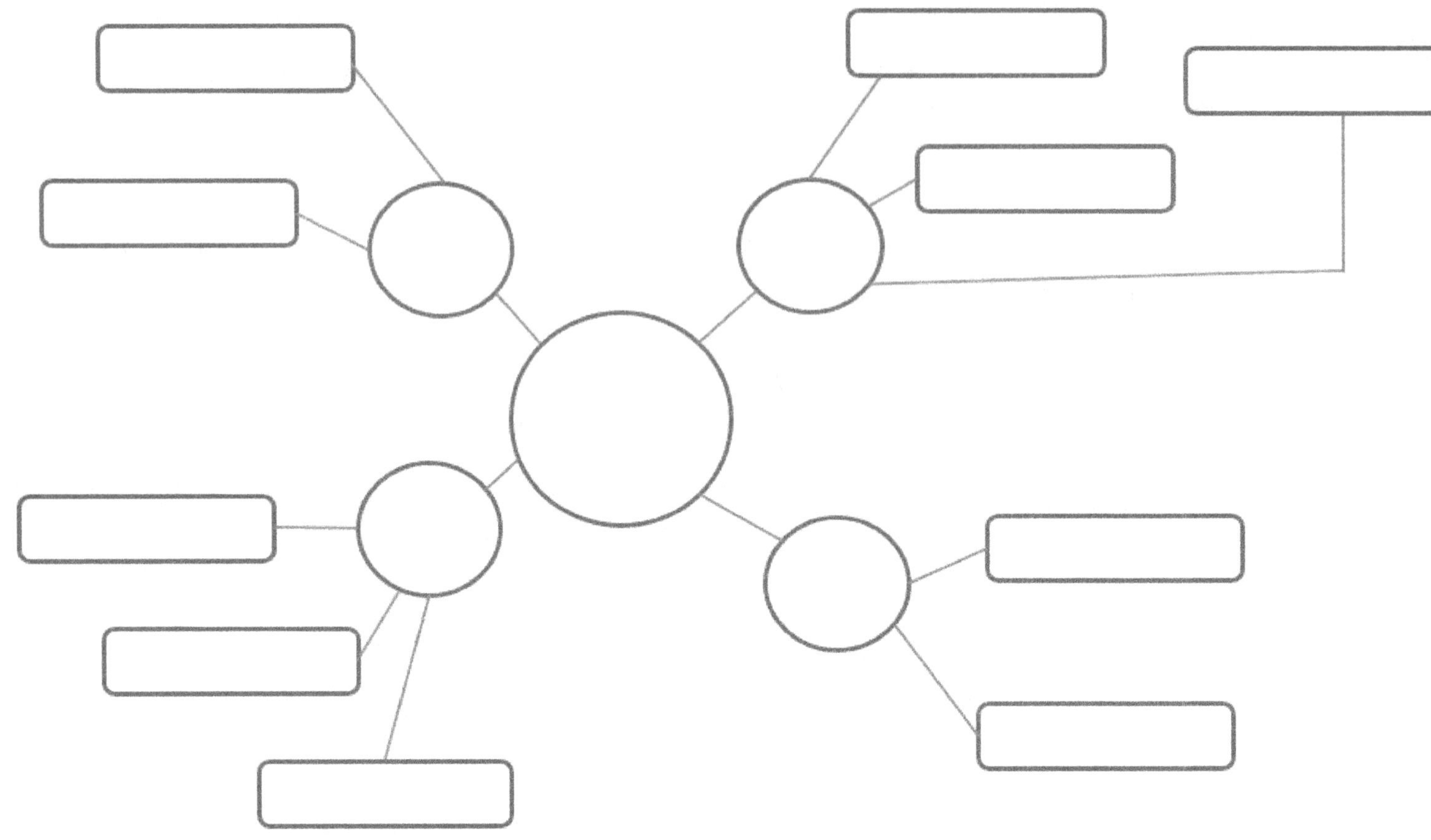

Academic Writing: As Easy As 1-2-3 by J. Nathan Garrett

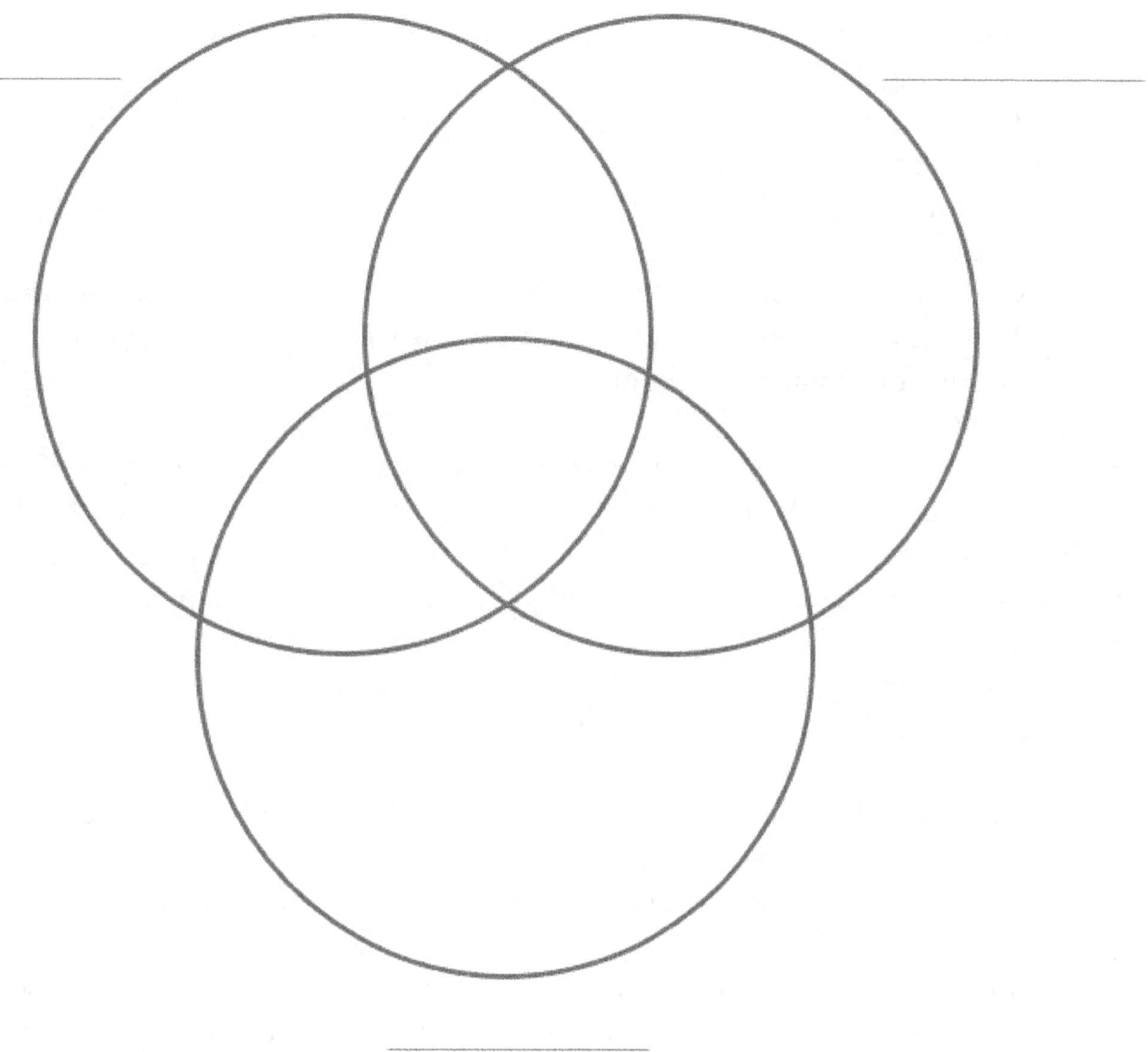

Academic Writing: As Easy As 1-2-3 by J. Nathan Garrett

THESIS STATEMENTS

Getting your thesis statement right is a great way to make sure your essay has the correct amount of focus and is doing what you intend it to do. The thesis statement has the following duties:

1. Be a road map for your paper's reader – it will tell your reader what to expect from the rest of the paper.
2. Answer the question or fulfill the purpose of the essay – not just be a statement of the subject.
3. Makes a claim about something, which others might be able to argue with.
4. Be contained in a single sentence located, usually, at the end of your introductory paragraph/section.

So let's say your essay is to be a persuasive essay about your favorite type of food. Your thesis statement should tell your reader what your favorite food is and why. Or perhaps your essay is to describe significant event in history. Your thesis statement should name an event and say what about that event makes it significant.

Let's do some examples. Read the thesis statements below and consider if you can tell exactly what the essay is about and what it is trying to do.

1. The Chernobyl nuclear meltdown in 1986 caused severe environmental damage, served as a warning tale about mismanagement of nuclear power, and delayed the world's adoption of nuclear power for several decades.

2. Authentic Japanese ramen is my favorite food because it is cheap, has so many delicious varieties, and is good for you if eaten in reasonable quantities.

3. People are moving out of California because of high taxes, an intrusive and aggressive state government, and spikes in all kinds of crime.

Can you tell *exactly* what the essays are not only going to be about, but what they're trying to do? Can you also predict the structure of the essays?

Academic Writing: As Easy As 1-2-3 by J. Nathan Garrett

Your thesis statement should be able to do the same things! Let's take our Taylor Swift example from earlier. "Taylor Swift is the most important recording artist today…"

What do we have there? We have a statement that can be argued with! Hooray! But our thesis statement isn't complete. We need to briefly state why we think this is the case – and three main ideas to support your thesis's position are a good number to work with, especially for a five-paragraph academic essay.

So let's keep going: "Taylor Swift is the most important recording artist today because she's been in the public eye for fifteen years and is still going strong, she writes and records her own songs, and her popularity amongst listeners and critics is stronger than ever."

Now, how do we come up with an effective thesis statement? We build it, of course! Let's take one of our thesis statements from above and dissect it, shall we?

<u>Authentic Japanese ramen is my favorite food</u> because it <u>is cheap</u>, <u>has so many delicious</u>
           position statement   main idea 1   main idea 2

      <u>varieties</u>, and <u>is good for you if eaten in reasonable quantities</u>.
                    main idea 3

First off, we have the position statement, which is usually a statement of opinion or a statement of an event or other subject area. Say it simply and clearly, using specific language.

Then this thesis statement has three 'main ideas.' Having three main ideas to support your position statement provides an excellent structure for the common academic essay. So that's great! But also, the three main ideas should be stated in similar ways. Look at the main ideas in the dissected thesis statement above. Each is a complete thought and is nearly a complete sentence, having the same structure – starting with a verb that can use the 'it' as the subject of that sentence.

This is key! Make sure your main ideas in the thesis statement have the same structure. Go look at the other thesis statements listed above. Do the main ideas all have the same structure? Are they all adjectives? Nouns? Noun phrases? Clauses?

Academic Writing: As Easy As 1-2-3 by J. Nathan Garrett

They do, because we know what we're doing. Exciting, right?

At this point, you should have a pretty clear grasp of what a good, effective thesis statement looks like. But you might still be wondering how to make your own. If that's the case, try the following steps:

1. Look through your brainstorming notes and/or organizers for a topic, an idea, or a position that you feel most drawn to.
2. Figure out how to make a statement that expresses what you want to express. If you are most drawn to your notes about tigers, figure out what you want to say about tigers. This might be, "Tigers are amazing." This might also be "Tigers are the most dangerous big cat on the Earth." Or something else!
3. Gather some main ideas that support your statement. "Tigers are amazing because they're man's best friend, they can swim, and they can jump a hundred feet." (Okay, important note: not all of those things are true.)
4. All of a sudden, you have a thesis statement!

Again, here's a complete thesis statement: "Academic writing is the best subject in school because it teaches me to organize my thoughts, helps me to understand my own thought process, and clarifies the relationships between different causes and effects."

Position statement + main supporting idea 1 + main supporting idea 2 + main supporting idea 3 = A Great Thesis Statement

Now it's time to get into the actual building of our essay. If you've done the work we've been talking about up to here, prepare yourself to be pleasantly surprised about how easy this is!

Academic Writing: As Easy As 1-2-3 by J. Nathan Garrett

INTRODUCTION PARAGRAPH

The time has come to start building your essay. Of course, this will require some writing, but remember that writing has two phases: the first draft where you figure out what you're trying to say and later drafts wherein you are figuring out how to say that for readers.

In other words, your first draft is you telling yourself what you're thinking and figuring all of that out, and the second draft is you finding better ways to say that to anyone who reads your essay. So don't plan on getting it perfectly right your first time around! You have permission to have your first few tries be less than perfect. In fact, you won't find much in the way of perfect writing outside of *To Kill a Mockingbird*.

Now, let's get started on the Introduction Paragraph. Here's the part of the visual from the beginning of this workbook that applies to the Introduction Paragraph.

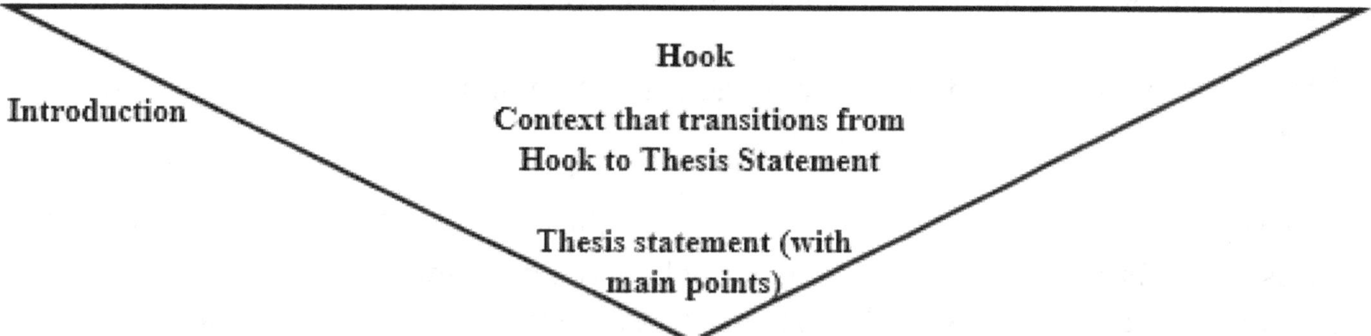

There are three components to an effective Introduction Paragraph:
1. The Hook – a sentence designed to 'hook' your reader's interest, and entice them to read your essay.
2. Context and transition (or the filler) – two or three sentences, usually, that transition from your hook to your thesis statement.
3. Thesis statement – you already have this ready, so you're a third of the way there!

Academic Writing: As Easy As 1-2-3 by J. Nathan Garrett

The Hook

The main thing to watch out for when composing your hook is to not use a sentence that is too outlandish. The hook's job is to entice the reader to keep reading, but not be so random and surprising that it has very little to do with your essay, and more particularly, with your thesis statement.

So the best approach to writing your hook will be to put yourself in the shoes of your reader, but also to stay in your own shoes. What do you find interesting about your topic and essay? What drew you to write about this? What do you think will capture a reader's attention?

Some things to consider for your hook: an interesting fact or statistic, a strong statement, a thought-provoking question, a brief related anecdote, or a related quote from a significant person. Here are some examples:

"Have you ever thought about who the most important music artist of the modern time is?"

"Alfredo Einsteino once said that ramen was the best food on planet Earth."

"The Chernobyl disaster delayed the world's adoption of nuclear power by at least thirty years."

Your best bet for crafting a good hook is to… brainstorm! That's right, start writing ideas down for what you could use for a hook. Write up to ten ideas down as quickly as your brain and fingers will allow, then choose from those. Remember that you want a captivating hook that you can connect with your thesis statement with two or three sentences.

Context and Transition – The Filler

The context and transition sentences might be the more intimidating part of the introduction paragraph. How are you supposed to connect your hook to your thesis statement. Well, your best bet is to take it step by step and to keep it simple. Write a simple, straightforward sentence that takes you one step from your hook toward your thesis statement. Then write another simple sentence that does the same, taking you another step closer. Then do it again. By now, you're probably well-transitioned to your thesis statement. Here's what that might look like.

Academic Writing: As Easy As 1-2-3 by J. Nathan Garrett

Alfredo Einsteino once said that ramen was the best food on planet Earth. Some people might argue with that statement. Others might think it goes a little far. But I believe that Mr. Einsteino was right. Authentic Japanese ramen is my favorite food because it is cheap, has so many delicious varieties, and is good for you if eaten in reasonable quantities.

That's a very simple example, so let's do another one, this time a little more complex.

The Chernobyl disaster delayed the world's adoption of nuclear power by at least thirty years. At the time that the Chernobyl nuclear plant was functioning, it was producing 1,000 megawatts of electric power, or 10% of Ukraine's electricity. This rate of production was impressive, given the newness of the process of producing electricity by nuclear means. But all of the good that the plant was doing was ultimately forgotten for decades after the disaster. The Chernobyl nuclear meltdown in 1986 caused severe environmental damage, served as a warning tale about mismanagement of nuclear power, and delayed the world's adoption of nuclear power for several decades.

Do you see how you can use logical, connected sentences to transition from your hook to your thesis statements? This will take practice and will also take you allowing yourself to write less than perfect first and second, and maybe more!, tries. Just keep going! Write one, then two, then three and you're there.

You might need a break at this point, and we recommend you take one. Do something active like taking a walk or playing some pickup hoops. This will both relax and stimulate your brain. So, take a breather, but not for too long! And when you get back to work, be sure to reread your work so far, including your notes and organizers.

Then it's time to jump into body paragraphs. Don't be too worried, you've already got the first sentence practically written!

Academic Writing: As Easy As 1-2-3 by J. Nathan Garrett

BODY PARAGRAPHS

The body paragraphs of your essay are where the rubber meets the road. This is where you expand on your thesis statement and arrange all of the thoughts and details and notes you came up with into something that will be enjoyable to read and will convince your reader that you're right.

Here's a visual of how your body paragraphs will work.

Body

Body Paragraph 1

1. Topic sentence (refer directly to first main point mentioned in the thesis statement)
2. Support 1 (can be one sentence or more)
3. Support 2 (can be one sentence or more)
4. Support 3 (if needed, can be one sentence or more)
5. Concluding sentence that drives the point home

Body Paragraph 2

1. Topic sentence (refer directly to second main point mentioned in the thesis statement)
2. Support 1 (can be one sentence or more)
3. Support 2 (can be one sentence or more)
4. Support 3 (if needed, can be one sentence or more)
5. Concluding sentence that drives the point home

Body Paragraph 3

1. Topic sentence (refer directly to third main point mentioned in the thesis statement)
2. Support 1 (can be one sentence or more)
3. Support 2 (can be one sentence or more)
4. Support 3 (if needed, can be one sentence or more)
5. Concluding sentence that drives the point home

Academic Writing: As Easy As 1-2-3 by J. Nathan Garrett

So, remember how your thesis statement has three main ideas to support your position? Those main ideas will become the guides for each body paragraph. Let's dig into that right away.

Body Paragraph Structure

In a traditional five-paragraph academic essay, your three body paragraphs can each follow the same structure. In fact, it's expected that they will follow the same structure. They don't have to be the same size or have the same number of sentences, but it won't be a problem if they do.

As you can see in the visual above, there are three main parts of the body paragraph. The topic sentence kicks things off, followed by several support sentences. The body paragraph will then close with a strong concluding sentence.

Let's start with the topic sentence. The topic sentence controls the whole paragraph and needs to state a single, complete thought that you can expand on in the paragraph. We cannot overstress the important point that the topic sentence must state only <u>one, complete thought</u> that you add additional thoughts and details about in the paragraph. Sometimes we try to do too much with our topic sentences, so stay focused on one, complete thought.

Now, the topic sentence comes directly from your main ideas in the thesis statement. In fact, the first main idea in your thesis statement will essentially become your topic sentence in your first body paragraph. Let's look at how that will work by looking at one of our previous thesis statements.

"The Chernobyl nuclear meltdown in 1986 <u>caused severe environmental damage</u>, *served as a warning tale about mismanagement of nuclear power*, and delayed the world's adoption of nuclear power for several decades."

The underlined section is the first main idea, so it will become the topic sentence of the first body paragraph. Like so:

"The Chernobyl meltdown caused severe and lasting environmental damage."

Academic Writing: As Easy As 1-2-3 by J. Nathan Garrett

As you can see, you can use the phrase right out of the thesis statement and work it a little bit to make a good topic sentence. That was fun! Let's do it again, but this time with the italicized portion, which is the second main idea.

"The devastating Chernobyl disaster also served for years as a warning tale about mismanagement of nuclear power."

You don't want to have your topic sentences all sound the exact same – that's just lazy writing – but they can have a similar structure. Just plan on using good transition words such as 'additionally,' 'furthermore,' and others that can help move your argument forward.

Next, you have your support sentences, which you should use to expand on your strong topic sentence. These should not be simply repetitions of what you've already said, but should add more information, more support, more details, and more interest to your essay.

Let's build a body paragraph using the first topic sentence we have above!

"The Chernobyl meltdown caused severe and lasting environmental damage. This was because for the ten days following the explosion, the reactor spewed radioactive materials extensively. These radioactive materials landed on roads, agricultural areas, and in bodies of water. Because of this radioactive contamination, people and animals were unable to continue living in the area, along with other adverse health effects, such as birth defects and illness. <u>Ultimately, while the contamination is being washed away by rain and other natural cycles, there are still areas of Russia, Ukraine, and Belarus where radiation levels remain too high for safety.</u>"

The underlined sentence is the concluding sentence. It offers a little more detail presented in a way to leave a strong impact on the mind of the reader. Usually, you can take one of the details you had come up with earlier in this process to build your concluding sentence around.

Now that we have one solid body paragraph, we just need to write two more using the same approach and we are ready to finish our essay with a solid concluding paragraph!

Academic Writing: As Easy As 1-2-3 by J. Nathan Garrett

CONCLUDING PARAGRAPH

Take a close look at the visual below. Do you see how it's pretty much the reverse of the introduction paragraph? A good concluding paragraph brings your essay full circle and leaves your reader with a complete and satisfying message.

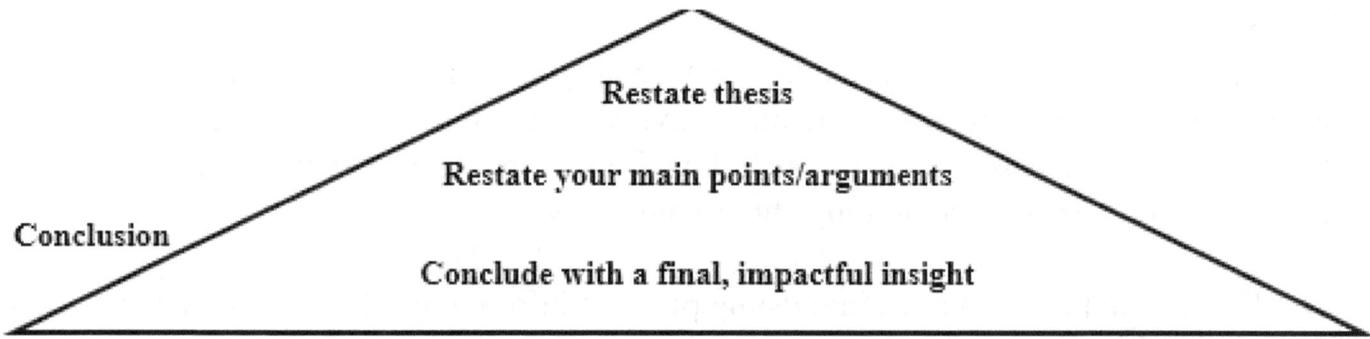

You will build your concluding paragraph by first restating your thesis. Restating means to say the thesis in a new way. Let's take our Chernobyl thesis statement and restate it to show how this will work.

First, here's that thesis statement again:
"The Chernobyl nuclear meltdown in 1986 caused severe environmental damage, served as a warning tale about mismanagement of nuclear power, and delayed the world's adoption of nuclear power for several decades."

We can restate it quite simply, usually by using a good summary phrase, such as "in conclusion," or "as we can see." Here goes:

"In conclusion, the Chernobyl disaster had far ranging effects on the area and the world that are not easily forgotten."

Next, we can restate our main ideas. This doesn't mean we copy and paste our topic sentences, but we can do what we just did with our thesis statement. Don't be afraid to be creative as you do this! Here's one way we might restate our main ideas for our concluding paragraph.

Academic Writing: As Easy As 1-2-3 by J. Nathan Garrett

"In conclusion, the Chernobyl disaster had far-ranging effects on the area and the world that are not easily forgotten, not the least of which being long-lasting environmental damage. Additionally, given that the meltdown was due to human error, we can learn a lot about how mismanagement of nuclear plants is the greatest danger from these otherwise safe sources of electrical power. Unfortunately, one of the greatest negative effects of the Chernobyl disaster was all the bad press that nuclear power got for decades after."

So now we have most of our concluding paragraph. Which means we're almost done with our five-paragraph academic essay. All that's left is to add what we like to call the Kicker. This is a final, concluding thought that leaves an impression on the reader and keeps them thinking about your essay.

The Kicker can present a new, interesting piece of information. It can also be a call to action. Whatever you decide to do, remember that you might need a few tries to find something you like and that works well.

Here's our complete concluding paragraph for Chernobyl.

"In conclusion, the Chernobyl disaster had far-ranging effects on the area and the world that are not easily forgotten, not the least of which being long-lasting environmental damage. Additionally, given that the meltdown was due to human error, we can learn a lot about how mismanagement of nuclear plants is the greatest danger from these otherwise safe sources of electrical power. Unfortunately, one of the greatest negative effects of the Chernobyl disaster was all the bad press that nuclear power got for decades after. Hopefully, now that the effects are fading, states and nations around the world will explore the nuclear power option as a safe and useful option for clean power."

And with our concluding paragraph done, that brings us to the end of this workbook. If this were an essay, I would restate the thesis statement, then make sure to leave you with a killer kicker.

But this isn't an essay. It's just your magical workbook that will help you become a wizard with essays. What you can do, now that you have a complete essay, is tell your friends about this beautiful workbook and maybe get a few copies for your friends, enemies, and family. And tell teachers.

Academic Writing: As Easy As 1-2-3 by J. Nathan Garrett

Also, leaving a review of this book and other wonderful content you use helps independent publishers like us do better. Thank you so much!